Ultimatum from Paradise

Ultimatum from Paradise

Poems

Jacqueline Osherow

LOUISIANA STATE UNIVERSITY PRESS)(BATON ROUGE

Published by Louisiana State University Press
Copyright © 2014 by Jacqueline Osherow
All rights reserved
Manufactured in the United States of America
LSU Press Paperback Original
First printing

Cover image: Copyright © Casa Batlló, 2014.

Designer: Barbara Neely Bourgoyne
Typeface: Calluna

My thanks to *Academy of American Poets' Poem-a-Day, Antioch Review, Epiphany, Jewish Daily Forward, Michigan Quarterly Review, New Ohio Review, Ocean State Review, A Poetry Congeries, Poetry Daily, Poetry International, Shakespeare's Sisters* (chapbook from the Folger Library), *Southwest Review, Western Humanities Review, Tikkun,* and *Zeek,* where some poems in this collection first appeared.

My gratitude to PEN Flanders, Eastern Frontier Art Foundation, the University of Utah Vice President's Office for Research, and the University of Utah College of the Humanities for their invaluable support.

I am grateful to Barry Weller for his help with this collection and to Brooke Hopkins (1942–2013), whose close attention to these poems, as I read them to him aloud, provided tremendous support and inspiration.

Library of Congress Cataloging-in-Publication Data
Osherow, Jacqueline.
  [Poems. Selections]
  Ultimatum from paradise : poems / Jacqueline Osherow.
      pages ; cm
  ISBN 978-0-8071-5806-7 (pbk. : alk. paper) — ISBN 978-0-8071-5807-4 (pdf) —
  ISBN 978-0-8071-5808-1 (epub) — ISBN 978-0-8071-5809-8 (mobi)
  I. Title.
  PS3565.S545A6 2014
  811'.54—dc23

                                                        2014008008

For Magda, Dora and Mollie

Contents

White on White

after Kazimir Malevich

It's the sort of painting I could never stand—
a white square askew on a white background—

[handwritten: → modern art]

one more aesthetic incarnation
of that swindled emperor, naked again,

[handwritten (left margin): the emperor's new robe]

preening in his nonexistent clothes;
I'd lived in Florence—where painting breathes—

seen how inanimate materials
(gold beaten to dust, crushed-up jewels

[handwritten (left margin): slant rhymes & almost rhyme]

mixed for rich and lasting color with albumen)
could be converted into pure emotion,

how master after master after master
had willed a chapel wall of fresh wet plaster

to make the ephemeral hold still
alongside the godly, the impalpable.

Why would you paint a white square askew
on a white background when you could go

[handwritten (left margin): slant rhyme / looks like it should / Rhyme but doesn't]

anywhere at all, encompass anything?
If the world failed us, at least a painting

might offer us its aggregate of rapture.
I had a stake in this, longed to capture

a bit of it myself (though my materials
would be more modest, words instead of jewels)

3

or at least exhaust myself in the attempt;
I was a seasoned dreamer and I dreamt,

which sustained me for quite a number of years.
But even the most stubborn of dreamers

is forced to notice, sooner or later,
that the world understands itself without her

albeit flattering intrusion
and it's a meager place once illusion

in all its glory is exposed as sham.
Besides, I've squandered poem after poem.

Just think of all the treasure I've left stranded,
uncultivated, the unattended

but manifest allegiances in things,
how a presence, of its own accord, sings

right within my own field of vision
and I always fail to take it down:

the year the snow came late and the mountain
was suddenly a tour-de-force of ermine

white on the golden residue of aspens
(it's the winter slant of light that determines

the color of their fur and not the snow)
or a June hike—what?—fifteen years ago,

the mountainside a visual haiku:
five mountain goats on the last patch of snow

and I would leave them there, forgotten.
That is, until, by accident I wandered in-

to the wrong room at MOMA, turned around
to a white square askew on a white background

and there were my mountain goats on snow.
Kazimir Malevich had seen them too,

how white craves white, how what's askew
yearns for some congenial milieu

where it can lose itself, disappear.
Those stunning ermine that snowless year

were neon on the gold leaves' makeshift carpets,
thrilling to witness, but ideal targets

for even the most dull-eyed predator.
Better to secure a sound white square

however unremarkable, unsubtle.
A person has to settle for what's possible.

A white square on a white background, askew.
Five mountain goats on the last patch of snow.

Dusk in January, Salt Lake City

In a fallow season, the smallest change
offers up a momentary lifeline.
Tonight, it's the mountains' rose reflection
of whatever gives the sky this neon tinge
muted by a pale stockpile of snow.
The air itself is rose, I'm breathing rose,
trying on the mountains' rose disguise
even as the sky goes inky blue
around two outsized wings loping toward me,
gangly, but for a slow-motion grace:
down, up, down, up—deliberate, steady,
completely noiseless, though they come so close
I half believe I've caught the owl's wild eye
as he scans the landscape for easy prey.

is she the
easy prey?

Unexpected Ferry Ride to Spain

Iceland's Volcano Disrupts Air Travel
—headline, *New York Times*, April 16, 2010

Volcanic Ash Will Cause Spectacular Sunsets in Britain
—headline, *Daily Mail*, April 16, 2010

The moon's
a pale sickle
blade atop
a single star
balanced
on a stack
of colored
rectangles
(purple over
orange over
crimson over
gold) as if
God were
a child piling
building blocks

on the narrow
strip of water
that keeps
Portsmouth
from the Isle
of Wight,
His tottery
construction
for all His
storied will
any second now
about to topple

and I only see
this because
the Earth's in
flux, spewing
its freshest
bits of rock
and glass
from a newly
temperamental
aperture,

wreaking
havoc with
our slim
pretense
of mastery,
our nonsense
about having
tamed the sky

when all along
we've been at
its mercy, as
I—for these
two nights
on the ferry
to Spain—am
at the mercy
of this fickle sea.

I'll awaken
on the Bay
of Biscay
to scour
the miserly
horizon for
whales and

dolphins who
will not show
themselves

as if to remind
me yet again
that above all
else the Earth
is mystery,
that our
movement
through it
must be slow—

a pilgrimage,
however
unconscious,
toward a
rumored
unremitting
majesty that
might at any
time reveal
its face:

a spout, a fluke,
a leap midair, a
moon over a star
over the show
of color put
on by the un-
seen overflow
of Earth's refusal
to contain itself,
that skyward
yearning we
call volcano.

Window Seat: Providence to New York City

My sixteenth
egret from
the window
of this train,
white against
the marshes'
shocking green
cushioning
Long Island
Sound from
Kingston down
to Mystic against
the shoreline's
erratic discipline:
the egret so
completely
still, the colors
so extreme,
the window
of my train
might be rolling
out a scroll
of meticulous
ancient Chinese
painting: my heart-
beat down its side
in liquid characters:
no tenses, no
conjunctions, just
emphatic strokes
on paper from
the inner bark
of sandalwood:

Structure is quick and easy to read & just like the train that flys by.

egret, marshes,
the number
sixteen: white
and that essential
shocking *green*—
perhaps even
the character
for *kingfisher*
green balanced
with *jade white*
in ancient poems—
every other element
implicit in the
brushstrokes'
elliptic fusion
of calm and motion,
assuring as my
train moves on
and marsh gives way
to warehouses
and idle factories
that my sixteen
egrets still remain:
each a crescent
moon against
an emerald sky,
alabaster on
kingfisher green,
its body motionless
on one lithe leg,
cradling its
surreptitious
wings

Penn Station: Fifty Years Gone

There must have been a train, a subway ride,
but what I remember is the palace
in-between: its high glass walls alive with light

and so enticing I thought closed-in space
more open, even, than open air,
light the only presence in the concourse,

though I must have seen throngs of women there.
Wednesday was Ladies' Day on the Pennsyl-
vania Railroad; women paid half fare

(a practice eventually declared illegal).
I was three or four and rode for free,
my unlucky sister stuck in school.

We did this often, my mother tells me—
Philly to Brooklyn in time for lunch—
and then the island on Eastern Parkway

where she sat with *her* mother on a bench
while I hopped from hexagon to hexagon,
examining the sidewalk, inch by inch,

for the secret of this new, compelling pattern
(molecule to petaled flower to star),
the quintessential feature of Brooklyn,

tightly fitted shapes nuzzling together
from Parkway pavement to bathroom floor.
Or did my notice of such things come after?

When we'd get there, as a family, by car,
the halfway mark in the Holland Tunnel
(whoever saw it first—always my sister—

awarded a nickel) arrival's sentinel,
next Liberty from the Manhattan Bridge.
But even she—torch and all—could not annul

that more and more impossible assemblage
of wrought iron, granite, glass and light
that gave me something of a sense of pilgrimage

a decade later in a window seat
on Amtrak, heading to a camp reunion.
My friends and I had arranged to meet

at the clock? information booth? in Penn Station,
then ride together to Valley Stream. . . .
I'd be face-to-face with stored-up vision

(how much was memory? how much was dream?)
what for years conspired in me to nurture
the sort of intimate, fanatic claim

we make as children on what we adore
and though I didn't know the terminology
my Platonic ideal of *architecture,*

unaltered, really, to this very day:
openness corralled and sealed with light.
But on that day in autumn 1970,

I got off the train to find concrete
and crowds and trash and ugliness and smell.
I assumed that in the interim they'd built

a slapdash addition to my beautiful
(perhaps too good to use?) remembered space,
found my friends and convinced them all

to join—did we miss a train?—my wild-goose chase
until finally we asked a policeman,
who told us this was all there was

when we asked for the "main part" of Penn Station.
Perhaps I was thinking of Grand Central?
an easy subway ride, just go down

that stairway, ride one stop, then take the shuttle. . . .
But it was late; we had to reach Long Island
before the Sabbath (we were under the spell

of Jewish summer camp) so I abandoned
one dream for another. Adolescents
are flexible that way. And our weekend—

hectic and euphoric and intense—
turned my confusion at Penn Station
into a funny story, its disappointments

postponed for our reunion's brief duration.
But on my train ride home, an acrid taste
pervaded everything: my initiation

into the recalcitrant mistrust
with which a bossy, noncompliant present
infiltrates and redesigns the past.

Still, I was, after all, an adolescent;
I had a world to change, a war to end,
and though I *knew* my vision wasn't

of any other station, I abandoned
my newly defenseless memory—
though I would have liked to understand

where it had come from; perhaps TV?
But my childhood TV was black-and-white
and I could see pink stone against a shimmery

golden-yellow amplitude of light
extending in every known direction. . . .
Only years later, as an undergraduate,

when the fate of Grand Central Station—
thanks to Jackie O's gift for publicity—
became a topic of dinner conversation,

did I finally unravel my old mystery.
Jackie's war cry was the demolition
of Penn Station in nineteen sixty-three!

I grabbed someone's paper, in which Penn Station
was described as "great," "noble," a "masterpiece,"
half-thrilled by this belated confirmation,

half-shamed at having betrayed my memories.
That light-struck little girl had not been wrong,
she and I the unsuspecting repositories

of the world's lost treasure—all along
(there's no overstating the world's recklessness
with what's irreplaceable) in our safekeeping—

and—or so it seemed—nowhere else.
Still, it was, at best, a Pyrrhic victory,
since there'd be no returning to my palace,

though I did have sightings: an illusory
thirty-five-millimeter meteor
flashing by me in *The Palm Beach Story*

(in those days, we saw movies in the theatre),
The Seven Year Itch, Strangers on a Train.
And then, a real find, outside a bookstore

in the used-books rack? remainders' bin?
among the pages of photos in a cast-
off coffee-table book of old Manhattan:

wrought iron, stone and glass, possessed
by something more like sorcery than sun,
an image I suspect has long replaced

or perhaps just merged with? my childhood vision,
Berenice Abbott: *Penn Station Interior.*
Take a look, reader, it's online.

(Perhaps I should have told you this before?)
You can even buy a print: an aura magical
enough to turn a person, even at four—

especially at four?—elegiacal
for at least another half century—
which explains the, for me, irresistible

allure of train stations—call it my history—
the more gargantuan and whimsical,
over-the-top, absurd, unnecessary

the more I love them: Antwerpen Centraal
(Sebald's Austerlitz), Milan, St. Pancras. . . .
Forgive me, but, for all its grace, Grand Central

doesn't have the lushness to redress
what turns out to be my great childhood loss.
The place—after all—is steeped in darkness:

too much travertine, too little glass.
And yet, reader, I still thrill to go there,
famished as I am for any trace

of the notion that arrival or departure—
anyone's at all—is apt occasion
for unstinting outpourings of grandeur.

And there it is, reader—it's not *Penn Station:*
Interior by Berenice Abbott I see
but an entire universe's concentration

on the daunting task of welcoming me—
Jackie!—after my first ride on a train,
which—oh how memory breeds memory—

must have had a caboose, a little red one—
like the one in the story in the Golden Book
my mother surely read me on that train

(she made it an adventure to be stuck
at a railway crossing: *the caboose! look!).*
For a minute, I imagine she walked me back

to see the caboose on our train in New York—
but only freight trains had cabooses; wrong again.
Oh reader, forgive me, the nostalgic

wasn't my intended destination
but what can I do? I've been derailed.
I wanted to tell you about Penn Station—

so magical a place even a child
would claim it as her private, secret palace—
how I once inhabited a world

so benevolent, its public space
seemed to cherish every human being.
I honestly haven't thought of that caboose

for nearly fifty years (it wasn't among
the Golden Books I read to my own children;
perhaps they didn't reprint it?). I wasn't expecting

to be blindsided by my mother all of a sudden,
but she had a way of singling out
anything she thought might give her children

even a brief instant of delight,
must have reveled in my private store of marvels,
though I was sure I kept them secret.

She'd present the simplest things as miracles
(not that she could have known they'd turn elusive).
Have I managed to do that for my girls?

What will they half recall, half try to prove
in fifty years? With what tenacious
if hazy spectacle they've caught a glimpse of

(one I likely see as commonplace)
will I—or, rather, my memory—be entwined?
Just let it be wide-open and gratuitous,

evocative of something like the kind
of—what shall I call it?—solicitude?
that made me think the world had been designed

with only me in mind, my childhood
a string of wonders. With each fresh thing—
a stray leaf clinging to a piece of fruit,

a twin yolk in an egg, a cardinal idling
in our neighbor's birdbath: my mother's voice,
so urgent and excited we'd come running.

Back from the laundry, a pillow case
with a tiny Chinese character inside its hem
was bounty from an over-brimming universe

with a prize (*Cracker Jack* writ large) in every item.
No doubt it was she who pointed out
the way Penn Station's granite walls would gleam

in all that captured, concentrated light,
the roof of windows letting in the sky's
wide-open pathways, the infinite

just one among a host of possibilities
in a world so enthralling, so magnanimous
all you had to do was open your eyes

and you'd be swept up in a fast embrace
of deft if momentary harmonies,
an eleventh-hour glimpse of iron, stone and glass,
an ultimatum from paradise.

her beautiful" was mother made because it so

II

Art Nouveau: Brussels to Nancy

Victor Horta and Louis Majorelle

I

It's as if Goethe, on his deathbed,
were directing the not-too-distant future
of his dreamy continent's dreamy adventure
in dressing itself up; builders obeyed
his famous last requirement, "more light,"
the very instant it became possible.
A New-World concoction—reinforced steel—
meant an architect could newly dictate
entire walls composed only of glass,
that a dim and stuffy bourgeois drawing room
in an always overcast city like Brussels
might suddenly unleash its smothered glow
and with it sweep away a millennium
of European darkness. Art Nouveau.

II

From then on: light in Europe. Art Nouveau
would abolish darkness of every kind;
its founders meant their luster to extend
to class and poverty, establish new
and principled arrangements of society. . . .
How I love and envy them for thinking beauty
had that kind of influence, that pull
even if, for the moment, only rich people
could afford to put their ideals into practice:
a house with each component made by hand
to mimic nature, so that even a hat stand
has hooks with leaves and petals so precise
you recognize their species at a glance,
whimsy mesmerized by diligence.

III

Because it is whimsy. That too I love.
Why have a line when you could have a curve?
Why not cover every unused surface
with a mural or mosaic or a frieze,
that is, once you've given sufficient leeway
to the necessary transparent reverie
for filling every room with tinted light:
a preening peacock, a swallow midflight,
wisteria, silver dollar, pinecone, lily,
even a stylized sprig of local parsley,
ubiquitous and more or less a weed.
Do what you want, they cry, and what you need
will follow. Ours is art for everyone.
This on the very eve of World War I.

IV

But I've reached war too soon. I meant to bask
in the thrill of Art Nouveau a little longer,
to borrow its initial joy, to linger
over each obsessive detail, every risk
embraced in giddy thrall to innovation,
internalize its retro grace as new.
As usual I lack imagination,
can't pretend I don't know what I know—
how the century would break its promise—
though, needless to say, for some of us
—me, for example—it meant life, not death,
albeit life contorted by the aftermath
of the unassimilable years before,
their conclusive proof of who we are . . .

V

what these lucky dreamers didn't yet know,
which is why they could imagine that a window
in each internal wall within a house
would make light universally contagious.
Still, even Mister "More Light" himself
had understood the dark appeal of Satan;
perhaps his Faust was a premonition.
Though who could have foreseen what would engulf
his dimming homeland in a century's time?
Maybe the trick is just to dream
in spite of what you guess, or even know
in increments: say, steps that seem to float
upward toward an ever-spreading halo
of captured? rescued? liberated? light. . . .

VI

I climbed that curving stair again and again
in Horta's perfect house—now a museum—
but an embarrassment by nineteen fifteen
with all the corpses piling up in Belgium.
Excess and whimsy must have seemed obscene.
He sold it—I imagine—for a song.
Its moment hadn't lasted very long—
they'd probably have torn the building down
if they hadn't had so much else to build. . . .
But now just a glimpse of its façade
wreaking havoc with a city block
completely conquers me; I'm so ecstatic
I scour the city for more just such façades;
I've always been a sucker for what fades.

VII

And most *have* faded—some in dreadful shape,
some nearly crumbling, some boarded-up,
but each victorious in its private face-off
with its lackluster street's lackluster self,
each—though I'm searching for it—a surprise.
My map comes apart (it's pouring with rain)
but even after finding several dozen
I still do double takes, distrust my eyes.
Who knew structure could be unhinged
from every practical consideration?
What willful paradise have we shortchanged
by squandering each reckless invitation
from a blossom, a vine, a leaf, a bird,
a common weed, a poet's dying word?

At Peter Behrens' House

Mathildenhöhe, Darmstadt

Later, he'd join the Nazi Party,
but first, he was a member of the artist colony
at Mathildenhöhe, the dreamy folly

of Ernst Ludwig, Grand Duke of Hesse
(grandson of Queen Victoria), who thought progress
meant dedicating the hilly wilderness

at the sleepy edges of his sleepy capital
to a hand-picked group of artisans, whose skill
would establish there a wonderland of Jugendstil—

the German variant of Art Nouveau.
He'd join the Nazis later, but at Mathildenhöhe,
Peter Behrens glutted every craft show

with prototypes still cutting-edge today:
a svelte decanter, a fluid tea tray,
each asymmetric cup handle a lily

from a garland on a streamlined saucer's rim.
He would join the Nazi Party but in the interim
adorned his cottage with a massive trim

of thick ceramic brick in bottle-green.
Inside, each item made to his specification:
plate, lamp, carpet, fork, knife, spoon. He'd join

the Nazi Party. I don't speak German
but try to read the paragraphs of information
a total work of art?—totalitarian?—

Behrens didn't join the party until
long after he'd abandoned Jugendstil.
His true genius was the industrial:

his first such masterpiece: a factory
for turbines at the growing AEG
as it jumped headfirst into the brand-new century.

By midway through, it would use slave labor,
make turbines for the generator
at Auschwitz, while, at the call of Albert Speer,

Behrens produced a monumental design
for the Reich's vision of a New Berlin.
Peter Behrens would join the Nazi Party when

it was still illegal, in '33,
but before that he'd initiate Le Corbusier,
Mies van der Rohe *and* Gropius—the three

undisputed masters of the modern—
into the mysteries of their vocation.
Each one began his study of design

as apprentice to Behrens at his firm.
Who would think you could trace an axiom
like *less is more* or *function dictates form*

to a protégé of someone who began
as a mastermind of ornamentation?
We could put it down to revelation—

proof of the triumvirate's great genius;
but some say these were Behrens' own ideas,
his name abandoned in the dense morass

of his ugly allegiances in politics.
We wouldn't want a century's aesthetics
linked to the designer of a Nazi complex

even if they are no longer in vogue.
On the other hand, this Nazi ideologue—
as late as '29—designed a synagogue.

You can see it on the Web—it's in Zilina,
a little city somewhere in Slovakia—
still standing, though it's now a cinema.

They brag about it—a rare, modern
synagogue in Europe, its design
by—they don't say Nazi, they say German—

the important German architect: Behrens.
What else should we call a man whose vision spans
the seemingly unnavigable distance

from excessive curve to simple line?
Still, his was a singular straight line. . . .
Maybe there's no real contradiction.

It was radical aesthetics he embraced,
every new hyperbole compressed
by the rigid strictures of the stylized;

maybe all Behrens did was follow
stylization's obsessive arrow
straight to Bauhaus from Art Nouveau—

different exteriors, same core:
same all-or-nothing fervor, same allure
of the all-defining, elusive contour

only exaggeration renders visible.
He would join the Nazi Party, but not until
he'd reinvented design as industrial.

Even the clock, you know that quintessential
black-rimmed clock we had at school,
no-nonsense, ubiquitous, so simple

you never even thought it had an origin?
I saw its picture—a Behrens design.
Now, all I want to do is run

like some crazy person from school to school
and pull each goddamned clock out of the wall.
But who am I kidding?—the world is full

of Behrens'—albeit unacknowledged—legacy,
object after object of rare beauty.
Later, he would join the Nazi Party.

Fantasia: Charles Rennie Mackintosh

Begin with a square, an elongation
of a simple line until it's radical—
decoration as art; art as decoration—

the squat chair reborn as purely vertical,
as if a heron required a throne
and a whiff always of the heretical.

Even his one church has an undertone
of the sexual (the motif's a seed
in various stages of gestation)

and in Mackintosh's house the massive bed
was a holy of holies: white, enclosed,
an altar to a private, hybrid god

for whom the sensual was stylized.
Or perhaps to his wife, partner and muse,
whose gessoes and tapestries exposed

the curves that energized his angled surfaces.
Margaret Mackintosh, née Macdonald
(see her *May Queen,* her *White Rose and Red Rose,*

her huge *All ye that walk in Willowood*)
so loved the all-encompassing regime
the story is she served only white food

in her white floating cloud of a drawing room
with its cabinet modeled on a kimono—
a room much like the one described as *dream*

by a journalist-believer in Torino
at the first international exhibition
of modern decorative art—1902—

but dream emancipated by precision
from its customary camouflage of haze,
an indefatigable invitation

to an unprecedented paradise
where excess is unleashed and disciplined
by a foolproof conflux of obsessiveness,

audacity, genius and sleight of hand
harnessing implacable control
to faith that paradise *can* be contained

detail by fanatical detail.
Needless to say, a costly proposition.
Maybe it was nothing short of a miracle

that anyone ever took Mackintosh on—
wildly over-budget, behind schedule,
rejecting every hairline imperfection:

an exquisite made-to-order handrail
lacking a tiny essential curve,
a hand-made rug, with far too pale—

or was it too intense?—a reddish mauve
(the handrail was entirely remade
but Mackintosh managed to dissolve

the rug's offending color thread by thread,
each pulled out painstakingly by hand),
not to mention the verboten colored food. . . .

Some did refuse to build what he designed—
the Glasgow School Board changed details
of his new primary school for Scotland

Street—just south of the river—his black tiles
turned to white, his windows standardized,
his iron gratings replaced with handrails

on the stairs that nonetheless revolutionized
forever what the world's stairways would be:
towers—in Scotland's gloom—infused

with light, their shape borrowed from nearby
medieval fortress-castles, with their stone
replaced by concentrated energy

from a not otherwise obliging sun. . . .
The stairway encased in walls of glass
was one more Mackintosh innovation—

this one so extreme, so audacious
it became the definition of the modern
when copied eight years later by Gropius.

Just think of generations of children
(the school remained in use for seventy years)
associating everything they'd learn

with clambering up light-bedazzled stairs.
How I envy them, taking for granted
what feel to me like such exotic pleasures,

their math and spelling drills daily supplanted
by daydreams built on tile-work designs'
eccentric polygons, newly undaunted

by geometry's insipid limitations.
Am I romanticizing? Perhaps it's ruinous
to grow up surrounded by perfections.

Maybe the two girls raised in Hill House
(imagine coming home to that front hall—
Mackintosh's domestic masterpiece)

suffered all their lives from an insatiable
and unrelenting yearning after harmony—
every room they'd enter unendurable.

Unless they grew up to loathe the tyranny—
of that all-controlling—if sublime—décor.
Who knows? Perhaps they dreamed of disarray

as I, who grew up mired in disorder
(we only ever cleared our mess for *company*),
approach these ideal rooms with so much fervor—

though I'm not sure I take in the reality
that people lived like this from day to day.
Where was all their stuff? Life is messy.

Besides, wouldn't someone else's fantasy
become, after a while, a little much?
And Mackintosh's was so exaggeratedly

idiosyncratic in approach
it would—within a century—fall victim
to a still expanding industry of kitsch

(you can find virtually any item
in a "Mackintosh" motif offered for sale).
When function plays hide-and-seek with form

it leaves a designer highly vulnerable
to this sort of leveling distortion.
But the mistress of Hill House, meanwhile,

never made a single alteration
(she lived there fifty years) in its décor
except, in the year after construction,

for insisting on a full-length mirror
in her perfect bedroom, though the added height
obstructed the streamlined chandelier. . . .

I suppose each of us has a limit.
For George Bernard Shaw, it was sleep
in the guestroom at seventy-eight Derngate—

with its proto-op-art black-and-white-stripe
motif even on the ceiling (one more first).
I hope the décor won't keep you up

(so the anecdote goes), said Shaw's host,
to which the playwright famously replied
No. Luckily I sleep with my eyes closed.

But I'd give odds he lay there open-eyed
in all that black-and-white aggressiveness,
amazed, if nothing else, at the certitude

that could spur an artist to sacrifice
all hope of domestic quietude,
render him permanently oblivious

to what a living human being might need;
for Mackintosh control and excess
were the only latitude and longitude

with nothing in-between, no compromise.
Perhaps that's why, in his final decade,
not one of his designs was put to use.

He did watercolors, drank, finally died.
But, years later, his quintessential designs
are almost universally applied. . . .

Even Ikea and Target borrow the lines
of his high-and-narrow-backed dining chair . . .
and in Glasgow, they've fulfilled his plans

a century or so late—for House for an Art Lover;
architectural monument-cum-reception hall
(they were setting up a wedding when I was there),

but to me it's missing something palpable—
Mackintosh would never have stood
for those kitschy gessoes, those lackadaisical

designs in the fabric and the wood. . . .
There's no sign of the hypervigilance
that for him constituted artistic method.

Or maybe what was needed was his presence
(with Margaret's for the fabric and the gesso).
For Mackintosh, design was performance

as composer, maestro *and* virtuoso,
with sound metamorphosed into place,
an unplayable *presto furioso*

like the finale of the A-minor Caprice
which, according to tradition,
brought down every European concert house

(even Glasgow's in 1831)
when Paganini himself performed his piece—
unrepeatable but sure perfection

as if he controlled a flawless universe
at least for its fugitive duration.

Dream Snapshots, Tel Aviv

I

How this shameless,
self-possessed cabal
of trees—poincianas,
oleanders, jacarandas—
and their loudmouth
sidekicks, the bougainvilleas—
must flabbergast these
nervous little streets,
not to mention their
luftmensch namesakes,
a tri-millennial backlog
of monomaniacs, poets,
crackpots, rabbis,
schnorrers, dreamers,
for some of them,
these selfsame
streets the dream—

II

or not these selfsame
streets—no, not quite
these, that is, if they
got to streets at all.
I doubt they broke
things down to such
particulars, so focused
were they on the larger
picture, streaked though
it was with streams
of honey, milk and
grapes too large
for one lone
man to carry.

III

Could there be a more
unlikely spectacle?
Pale, round-shouldered
connoisseurs of argument
picnicking beneath
these neon trees. . . .

IV

And behind these trees:
the dated future,
imagined into concrete
in the brutal nineteen
thirties by refugee
protégés of Gropius,
intent on making,
even in the back-
ward, hot Levant,
a white, clean
egalitarian promise.

V

(It's a Bauhaus fairyland,
Tel Aviv's White City,
declared a World
Treasure by the very
UNESCO whose orange
paper boxes I left
penniless on Halloween—
though used to saying "trick
or treat for UNICEF"—after
one of my parents' many
Jewish organizations
accused the fund of
anti-Israel bias.)

VI

Perhaps the would-be
architects embraced
their exile—an entire
city to be fashioned
out of nothing!—envisioned
themselves as sleek,
no-nonsense avatars
of the Baroque masters
of Noto and Ragusa,
conjuring splendor
out of thoroughgoing
disaster, each town
leveled by Etna
newly bodied forth
with unsurpassable
jewel-box grace.

VII

Only this time
the disaster
was miles away.
Clearly, there
had been no lava
flow at this form-
follows-function
seaside outpost,
no eruption, in fact,
of any kind, unless
it was the designers'
forced arrival (not
that another place
on earth would
have them) but
how could they
have attempted

(especially in this
piece of the world)
a construction that
*would one day rise
toward the heavens?*

VIII

Besides, how did they
miss the tenacious
towers and walls
of the ancient city
already here, from
which Perseus (with
the aid of winged
sandals borrowed
from Hermes) is said
to have freed the chained
Andromeda (signs
point out the very rock)
and the wingless and
presumably friendless
Jonah (a friend would
no doubt have talked
him out of it) bought
his passage on
the luckless ship
upended by his ill-
considered getaway?

IX

Those people I
was having trouble
picturing beneath
these trees could
have recited his entire

story by heart, as well
as the one about the
drastic repercussions
of trying to build a
tower to the heavens.
They'd learned them
in a dingy schoolroom
by the age of six—but
not about Andromeda
or names of trees
or what a person
near a sea would
need to know.

X

They rarely saw the sun,
much less an ocean . . .
and, though they'd
never once been any-
where near this spot,
knew a host of similes
for their *return,* my
favorite (I, too, know
at least some of them
by heart): *as flash floods
gushing through the desert.*

XI

I'm sure they
never dreamed of
Jewish beaches,
lorded over by luxury
hotels, with views of
*daughters of Jerusalem,
ornaments tinkling*

not just *on their feet*
but in their belly buttons,
shockingly visible
everywhere you turn
between their flimsy
smidgeons of bikinis . . .

(though there is—God
be praised—a walled-in
section, which would
no doubt have enraged
progressive dreamers,
for women on odd,
men on even days . . .)

XII

and all-night groceries,
internet cafés, night clubs,
strip clubs, video arcades,
always a conundrum
to squeeze a dream
into the pockmarked
confines of the actual

XIII

even before we consider
the people whose opposing
dreams boast a deep
knowledge of the local
flora . . . some of
whom remember
taking for granted
the scent of jasmine
as it commandeered
the slow, lackluster breezes

pampering the courtyards
of their not yet ruptured
childhoods before
they could distinguish
its perfume: the air itself
a well of unacknowledged
sweetness on those
long since cut-off
summer afternoons.

XIV

What a pity
recompense
is so illogical
in its fitful
and exacting
expectations:

an infinity
of justified
petitioners
so hell-bent
(desperate?)
on getting
payment,
they don't put
too fine a point
upon its source

XV

and end up wreaking
havoc on susceptible
and inauspiciously
positioned bystanders
who, as they survey

the expanding wreckage
from their new
and godforsaken
vantage points, will
themselves clamor
until they, too,
secure their share
of misbegotten rewards.

XVI

I too have a taste
for all or nothing—
but maybe now
the wildest choice
is compromise.

Unlikely as it is,
this city's here—
and, forgive me,
forgive me, but
I couldn't say
I'd prefer this
skewed, unseemly
world without it

XVII

any more than
I'd have preferred
pristine Manhattan,
before it succumbed
to what appears to be
its inherent weakness
for gaudiness

XVIII

though I admit
to taking solace
in the amplitude
of the messy
intervening years
since that crucial
round of swindling
took place.

XIX

No such luck with
this upstart city,
and its blinding spread
of blooming promenades,
soon to be covered over
in magenta, lavender,
orange, yellow, mauve
and purple petals,
some of which may flutter
to the doggedly futuristic,
if seventy-year-old,
asymmetric balconies
of airy apartments
that have not kept
their innovators'
visionary promises.

XX

Let me tell you
something: I've
seen flash floods
in the red rock
of my adopted

Southwest desert,
the stark, stark cliffs
suddenly hysterical
with waterfalls,
setting off rainbow
after rainbow
like strobe lights
in a discothèque, as
regular and strange
as that, flashing *red*
orange yellow green
you're dizzy, but you
know what's coming: God's
blue indigo violet
promise: no destruction.

XXI

So who's to say
those flash floods
to which we're
likened in the psalm
aren't in fact encoding
an injunction? It's late,
I know, but can't
we cut our losses?
Learn something from
the pyrotechnics
arcing off the desert's
floods, or even this
ROYGIBV converging
in these trees, God's
hand-made protest
banners: no destruction

XXII

or maybe we
can learn it from
the hard-nosed dream
still thrumming
through these sun-
baked slabs of concrete—
nothing less (at least
according to the Bauhaus
manifesto) than *creative
activity's ultimate aim!*
Too bad their *million
workers* (no *class
distinctions . . . between
craftsmen and artists*)
were so narrowly
imagined; they forgot
ethnicity, nationality,
religion (in Germany
1919), too busy, I guess,
dreaming up their *new
and coming faith:
architecture, sculpture
and painting in a single
form.* It's as if they'd
set out to copy those
people of the plains
of Shinar: unity
the other Babel error.

XXIII

Unless we've been
misreading the story
all these years; it's
a matter of God's

distaste for hearing
the same words
over and over, His
desire for multiplicities
of language, each
with its private armory
of eloquence, precision,
its own eccentric genius
for delusion. Maybe
He's a proponent of
the Bauhaus version
of the tower, despite
its aspiration *toward*
the heavens. He too
is an idealist, dreaming
of a no-frills paradise
where anyone and
everyone can come,
a spare, white sanctum
where holiness inheres
in light and air and
ample room.

Love Song to Antoni Gaudí

Build me a lightwell; tile it deepening blue;
tend me a cathedral's open forests;
conjure me mosaics out of broken
pieces of ceramic over undulating
fireplaces, windows, doorframes, walls;
give me blue, shafts of blue, waves of blue.

Position the lightwell so in spots it's seen
only through distorted sheets of glass,
rippled so the blue tile swells to ocean,

the cathedrals, so mosaics shout *hosanna
in excelsis* and *sanctus sanctus sanctus*
from bell towers that might be tentacles
of vast deep-sea creatures in exile
sloughing off the ocean's strict ubiquity
on rumors of the pliancy of sky.

But why this importuning? It's all here
so like the havoc of hallucination,
I half think it originates with me—
whoever that is—I've lost all certainty—
can't separate my longing from Gaudí's

even if I do misread his parables:
for example, that tentacled cathedral's
interior's not forest but oasis;
those slim bare trunks are clearly palms'—
crowned, in gold leaf, on the ceiling's vault
with fronds I take for disembodied wings

shed—it *is* a house of God—by angels.
But a tour guide reminds me that Gaudí
only copied what he'd seen in nature
or what—with their newly fine-tuned microscopes—

scientists had trained themselves to see—
hordes of structures: atoms, molecules
emerging from the dimness to disclose
matter's surreptitious agitation.

Still, all evidence suggests Gaudí
was most enamored of the information
he could summon with a naked eye
attuned to fine degrees of variation:
the subtle patterns in a reptile's skin
reborn as phosphorescent mosaic scales
in the outsized lizard fountain at the entrance
to the quirky, razzle-dazzle Park Güell
and the snake a little farther up the hill
uncoiling itself into a bench for lovers,

nannies, gossipers, exhausted tourists
some of whom have just come from the roof-
top maze of chimneys at La Pedrera
on the curved inversion of the curving ceilings
in the squat, arched attic rooms below
modeled on the ribcages of whales

while others are still reeling from the blue—
white to pearl to sea to sky to cobalt—
light-drenched arrow through the Casa Batlló

betraying every other earthly edifice
as, at best, a squandered opportunity,
at worst, an airtight substantiation
of the irreversible insolvency
of our close-fisted imaginations.

How we need you, Antoni Gaudí,
to gather us up single-handedly
inside the limitless, each dreaming room
spreading to embrace us like the cloak

(lapis lazuli with borders of gold)
the munificent *Madonna* we've
anointed *della misericordia*
opens to enfold repentant sinners.

Our sin here: the simple-minded reflex
to shut ourselves inside the rectilinear,
a contour wholly alien to nature
whose sole enclosed dwellings
—dovetailed hexagons for wasps and bees—
avail themselves of only obtuse angles

but a curator friend will interrupt
my sketchy theories about nature
and point me to the rising trunks of trees:

clearly, nature's lavish with right angles,
something I should certainly have noticed
in a poem paying homage to the architect
for whom *basilica* means *desert oasis*
teeming with the upright trunks of palms.

Still, for the most part, he liked to borrow
unpredictable clusters of angles
from the most unruly, expansive trees:
the Casa Batlló's asymmetric drawing rooms'
undulating windows fanning out
like branches on the spreading maple sycamores
shading curves of boulevards below.
Staring out, we're sparrows in their leaves,

each rise from lightwell to drawing room
on each successive floor of Casa Batlló
a metamorphosis from fish to bird
from sea to branch to sky to branch to sea.

I was wrong about those giant sea-creatures
whose tentacles you stole for your cathedral;
they revisit ocean all the time. . . .

You'd never limit a breathing animal
to just one insufficient element
in a universe as multiple as this
even as you fetishize details,

each of which would be enough for anyone:
one pillar like a bone, one like an elephant's foot,
a mushroom fireplace, a stained-glass shell,
a balcony that doubles as a falcon's nest
(its façade a cliffside in the wilderness),
another one a mask, one more a skull,

your plan for twenty-six spiral stairways
in your unrealizable cathedral
a would-be free-for-all of giant snails,

and your single incandescent mosaic lizard's
spine's wavy fringe of vehement blue
an intimation of the nearby ocean

like the tiled lightwell through the warping glass,
blurred to a heaving surge of blue—
sun through skylight mottling the waves,
its litany: *sanctus sanctus sanctus*
and *hosanna in excelsis,* residue
of long-forgotten rumors reemerging
(*am* I hallucinating? or are they true?):
darkness on the deep, wind on water,
light a revelation, startling, new,
interchangeable, the sea and heavens,
their blue-spangled goblets running over,
tongs of burning coals, rungs of angels,
rising and descending, blue on blue

Casa del Fascio

Giuseppe Terragni, 1932-36

I

Who knew light
was a construction
material? (the guard
tells me the basement
was a prison) that Giuseppe
Terragni's once Casa del
Fascio, now the local
ministry of finance,
is a right-angled
hierarchy of radiance:
small blocks, large panes,
rectangles and squares,
each an onslaught of
luminescence, pressing
through the ceilings, through
the stairwells, through the
walls, a Renaissance
courtyard only light
instead of marble, instead
of terracotta, instead of
travertine, the same intimate
dimensions intact, pristine,
only here each edge
is made of light

II

I wanted to see what
a Fascist thinks is
beautiful—though I
know, having read
in a trance the *Pisan
Cantos.* I loved

53

those flower petals
caught on stone
(bougainvillea, I always
thought), those clinging
leaves, that lyric overhaul
of still photography
Ezra Pound established
as his trademark: I even
used to love his early songs
before I found out ("spit on
the Jews for their money")
what was underneath
the thick black lines

III

I can't see anything
beneath this light
but fields of light,
their self-contained
treasuries of parallels
and perpendiculars
pieced together
in a taut mosaic,
partition in a nimble
truce with synthesis:
light meeting light
on grids of light

IV

The guard (by now
my best friend, having
let me in, not quite
according to regulation)
tells me about a woman
who comes here every

year, a woman ninety-
two, ninety-three, an ex-
partisan, once prisoner
in the basement, how
the two girls with whom
she was arrested faced
a firing squad. She comes
back every year to pray
on the anniversary of
the Allied victory, declared
as she awaited execution

V

I'd love to know
the substance
of those prayers—
have they changed
over the years,
or even from
the outset, skittered
from lamentation
to thanksgiving?
Surely they were
her friends, the
murdered girls?
Maybe it's penance,
a prayer for forgiveness
for her increasingly
obscene longevity—
or maybe it's not
prayer but sheer
bravado, the pleasure
of remembering her
would-be executioners,
strung up in a frenzy
by the crowd. Unless

it's something else
she'd remember:
the terror? ferociousness?
lack of imagination?
passion? stubbornness?
religion? whatever
turned into the where-
withal to bully fate
to give up another
day or two, another year

VI

Whatever she does
I doubt she sees
the architecture,
sublime though it is
(it is sublime). Still
without her noticing,
it works on her, that's
what scares me, even
in retrospect. What if
this were calculated
to blind us all, part
and parcel of its evil
purpose? What business
does a Fascist have
with light? and why am
I wholly susceptible?
I, who hate right angles,
hate the minimal,
who always thought
I hated modern
buildings: what chance
do I have—willing as I am
to fall beneath its
thrilling Fascist spell?

VII

Because, I'm telling you
it's dangerous—to say,
but still . . . to intervene with
words like grace and genius.
I don't favor execution
but I begrudge that bastard
Pound every last minute
in the madhouse

VIII

The guard tells me Mussolini
would stand right here,
right here, in the center
of light's clearinghouse,
his face a spreading rec-
tangle of glare. The guard
gets nervous, says it's time
to leave. But I ask questions,
keep him talking. I haven't
figured out what's going
on here yet, where the light
comes from, why it stays,
why every building in
the world doesn't glow
like this. This. This Fascist
House. I gaze and gaze.

III

Double Abecedarius

A cosmos ecstatic and abuzz
belies its scientists, and their crude theory,
conclusive though they claim to be, complex,
defining their approximations as "law."
Einstein was just engaged in improv,
fantasias from that gossamer milieu
generated by extravagant
hazarding of guess after guess,
imaginative, but not oracular,
judicious, perhaps, but still oblique.
Kabbalists come closer, in their deep,
labyrinthine inklings of a credo
mysterious in each deft navigation.
Never do they pretend to fathom
obscure dominions, though there they dwell,
pilgrims in a darkness where each dark
question is a stationary haj,
revelation a phony alibi,
secrets for them—however outlandish—
truth, which only flourishes in hiding,
ubiquitous but thoroughly aloof,
verification a devil's paradise—
warping the undefended mind,
exactitude instead an enigmatic
yearning after what we can't absorb.
Zero. Infinity. Abracadabra

Villanelle: Tikkun Olam

Repairing the World

Should I ask the obvious? Why would God
create a world requiring repair?
And what was He thinking when He called it good?

Unless *the perfect is the enemy of the good*
was His motto too. Maybe Voltaire
was making an obvious reference to God,

who clearly got in way over His head—
as if banning a piece of fruit was the answer,
not to mention thinking knowledge of good

and evil was the sin He should forbid.
My guess is He didn't imagine murder
until Cain made it obvious. Poor God.

No wonder He had that temper tantrum-cum-flood.
But He couldn't follow through, couldn't bear
to think of forfeiting whatever good

He had, albeit haphazardly, created
and so this somewhat slipshod world's still here.
Do you think *we* might do it any good?
Obviously, there's no point asking God.

Petrarch's 146: Yiddish Version

Your name—if my rhymes were understood
that far away—would fill Bactria and Thule,
Atlas, Olympus, Calpe, the Don, the Nile.

But since I can't reach all four corners of the world,
that lovely country will hear it that the Apennine
divides and the sea and alps define.
          —from Petrarch, sonnet 146

And in what scrap of earth will they hear my song?
Listen to my song? Which hills or seas
will take in all that shamelessness, that yearning?
And don't think by *song* that I mean this.
There's one—I barely understand a word—
lodged between my throat and my esophagus,
puffed up with endearments rarely offered
without some unsolicited advice,
its syllables: needles squabbling with thread,
the very ones that once sent me to bed
or told me I looked like my father's troubles.
They've left off, as they've left off scrounging rubles
(each curse a fresh disease, toothache or rash)
to eke out *kaddish* for their scattered ash.

A Crown for Yiddish

Antwerp: A Crown of Sonnets

I

Diamonds, Art Nouveau, Flemish bric-a-brac,
an inexhaustible supply of rain
and every once in a while, on a bike,
a black-suited, black-hatted, bearded man,
his hat made rainproof with a plastic bag
like the ones that dangle, bulging, from his handlebars.
At first I half think it's a sight gag,
that I've landed on some rain-drenched Jewish Mars,
but this is Antwerp, universal clearinghouse
for *the* commodity for people on the run—
and we're famous for leaving in a rush—
still harping on the bread we couldn't let rise . . .
which might explain the power of adaptation
of our other portable prized possession: Yiddish.

II

It's precisely for that prized, portable Yiddish
that I'm wandering around in this unlikely
city, where it's said against all odds to flourish.
Don't tell me there's Yiddish on Eastern Parkway;
I want it at its source: its native Europe.
Besides, the Brooklyn version is trumped-up—
a non-holy Jewish tongue. I pity the children
growing up with no real conversation
in a language their parents can only speak
so badly that I'm able to understand them—
I who possess such a modicum
of the language that I once earned the wisecrack
You speak Yiddish like a convert. (I was stung.
By rights, it should be my native tongue.)

III

By rights it should be my native tongue
and I can barely distinguish it from Flemish.
I'm eavesdropping, as I move among
the crowds in the diamond district. Yiddish!
on a cell phone no less! *A shanem dank*
he says it and I think it—a particular
I'll savor forever: *a shanem dank*
to you, black-hatted man: Yiddish cellular.
What Yiddish I have is from the phone;
my father-in-law at my house, after his stroke,
having more or less the same conversation
a dozen times time a day, better than a textbook:
the kids were spoiled, noisy, the house a mess;
his son was on him like the SS.

IV

They'd have come up sooner or later, the SS,
entangled as they were in the fate of Yiddish
and, as I'd find out from Hugo Klaus
(*The Sorrows of Belgium*), in part Flemish.
The SS Volunteer Verband Flandern
had a thousand Flemish volunteers,
not really a fact you want to learn
when you're on a search for Yiddish in Flanders
though—in retrospect—hardly a shock,
ambient hatred more or less a stock
component of Yiddish; it ricochets,
secreting in the simplest Yiddish phrase
a detonator with a short, short fuse:
that ragtag eloquence: nothing to lose.

V

A ragtag eloquence—nothing to lose—
but that's not accurate—there is *something;*
where else are you invited to confuse
pathos with precision comic timing,
suspect the gravity of any word,
turn it inside out, upside down?
ransack every language ever heard
for its choicest tidbits, make them your own
even—who else *is* there?—your enemies'.
No doubt a thousand years of constant quibbling
would give any language the expertise
to deflect incursions from the outside,
however vicious, however disabling—
that is, short of wholesale genocide.

VI

Once you mention wholesale genocide,
it seems obscene to focus on a language,
but words are palpable, unlike the dead—
and these the only remnants of my lineage,
that is, assuming that they do remain
beyond, say, the *messer, goppel, leffel*
confused with one another in my brain—
fork, spoon, knife interchangeable—
though how hard would it really have been
(*messer:* knife, *leffel:* fork, *goppel:* spoon)
to distinguish the components of the gibberish
happening around me all the time?
Though—who am I kidding?—do I really wish
this were a Yiddish, not an English, poem?

VII

This is an English, not a Yiddish poem
though my grandparents died of natural
causes, native Yiddish speakers all.
So the SS have to share the blame
for the fate of Yiddish with PS 63,
The Shadow, Betty Boop, the pledge of allegiance
that first-generation, go-getter diligence
my parents managed to pass on to me
that stopped on a dime with my children—
though I give their names the same diminutive
my father always tacked onto mine,
his exaggerated, head-shaking *Jakele*
inside my *Magdale! Dorale! Malkele!*
If a habit dies hard, will it survive?

VIII

If a habit dies hard, will it survive?
Should it? or is it pure sentimentality
that makes me long for Yiddish alive—
brings me to this ramshackle balcony
to sit among these women who won't show
their hair or let their female voices mix
with the men's below, my lone contralto
half protest, half involuntary reflex
since these are melodies I've always sung.
But who am I to say their rules are wrong?
What do I know? It works for them . . .
I forfeited my rights, rode the tram
to get here on this Holy Sabbath day.
How dare I sing along, pretend to pray?

IX

How dare I sing along, pretend to pray?
I've only come here hoping to listen in
to bits of Yiddish gossip *sotto voce,*
and then to hear my second Yiddish sermon.
My first was at sixteen: on Yom Kippur,
at the *shtibl* favored by my high-school crush;
zeyer a beautifuleh . . . is all I remember . . .
and the noisy women's section's sudden hush
when the rabbi announced the men's donations.
But the gossip here has French intonations,
the sermon's in Hebrew. I rise to leave
when the Cantor starts announcing the new month, Av,
with such intensity, I'm almost driven
myself to *love of Torah, awe of heaven.*

X

A life of love of Torah, awe of heaven
he repeats the line again again again
Life. Love. Torah. Awe. Heaven—
a fresh inflection with each repetition
as if to underline his words' pursuit
of what can't be captured, Torah and heaven
at once elusive and infinite.
Precisely this is what is to *daven—*
I'm getting my Yiddish lesson after all.
Why am I so astonished by the obvious?
that these scales and scales of notes per syllable—
exaggerated, even ridiculous—
keep a fragile universe alive.
Without them, the month might not arrive.

XI

Without them, the month might not arrive.
But then who wants it, the month of Av,
when we're meant to mourn, to fast and grieve
(our memories if nothing else survive)
for the destruction of the Temple in Jerusalem?
And yet his announcement gives me comfort.
Call me a sucker. It's what I am.
How else explain my thrill at every word
of Yiddish uttered on the Pelikaanstraat
as if it saved my essence from collapse?
But I hear little of it, I'm getting desperate.
Maybe, despite the *shtreimels* and skullscaps,
here, as in Brooklyn, Yiddish is stale:
mazel und bruche at a diamond sale.

XII

Mazel und bruche at a diamond sale.
Everyone says it—Christians, Hindus
(do Muslims trade diamonds?) when the sale is final.
They mistranslate and mangle the phrase
on the diamond museum's audio guide.
Luck and blessing, it means luck and blessing;
which seems to me a bit of wishful thinking
given the ugly source of what they trade . . .
and the traders so fastidious lest their food
(not just the Jews, but the vegetarian Hindus
whom I've seen eating kosher falafel and hummus)
be tainted with the smallest drop of blood.
But let's not go there. Business is business;
my survivor father-in-law owned a slaughterhouse.

XIII

My survivor father-in-law owned a slaughterhouse
for pigs in North Philly—he'd schlep carcasses
alongside his workers, local black guys
whom he turned into Shmulkes, Yankels, Moishes,
names they'd answer to, cutting him slack.
(He worked in short sleeves; they'd seen his arm.)
Besides, if you were thick-skinned, he had charm
though *this chicken is good, not like last week*
was the only sort of praise he'd ever give—
the birthright of a language whose first narrative
closes with a prayer to reach *Jerusalem*
or at least a village nearby. That Yiddish is gone.
How could it function here? It loathes the solemn.
I give up and cross the river for the skyline.

XIV

I give up and cross the river for the skyline
but here's a playground full of boys in yarmulkes
and girls in long skirts . . . their bright commotion
as they slide headfirst and crowd the monkey bars
so high-pitched and pristine, so sweet, so fresh
it takes me a minute to realize it's Yiddish—
the real thing. I barely make out a word,
it's as if my *bubbe* were on a sliding board—
though in my memory she's far more like
the gossiping mothers sitting on the bench.
There's no Flemish anywhere or even French.
Perhaps I'm dreaming this? When I come back
the few children here are speaking Arabic
beneath a skyline of Flemish bric-a-brac.

XV

One last diamond among the bric-a-brac,
our once ubiquitous possession: Yiddish
still breathing, still some children's native tongue,
despite modernity, despite the SS,
despite how much we've had to lose
(who can calculate the reach of genocide?).
Surely, one of them will write a poem—
habits die hard; poems survive—
will want to sing herself, not simply pray,
despite the allure of Torah, of heaven,
want a really new month to arrive,
a different kind of luck, a different blessing,
an end to slaughter, or at least a safe house
in a little town nearby, just past the skyline.

To Mary Sidney, on Reading Her Psalms

You give me a little courage, Mary
in your skittish dedication to her highness;
I too can *dare as humbleness may dare;*
if there's anywhere to speak with you, it's here
at the wordy Anglo-Saxon periphery
of the universe's one great surge of praise

though I'm lost here. Where's the joyful noise?
The clang of syllables I learned to memorize
before they were weighted down by meaning?
And what's all this complicated rhyme?
Don't mistake me—I'm not complaining;
it's just not my notion of a psalm

for all my love of wrought, elaborate things—
especially when they're the sort that sings
and yours do sing a stunning song—
but they're off-kilter without the awe
inherent in my ancient holy tongue;
I miss my *amen sela, hallelujah*

though I do applaud you and your brother—
going for the full linguistic bait-and-switch
in the move from one language to another:
David's disarmingly direct speech
a filigree of formal contrivance
(no form repeated more than once

in each of a hundred-fifty psalms!)
in your show-off/virtuoso hands.
Talk about *such a song in such a land*—
but what else is there in dreary England?
Its sole extravagance a trove of synonyms
that endlessly perplexes and expands

its mongrel, unbeautiful tongue—
a language, frankly, crying out for poetry
given its absence, even, of integrity,
not to mention intrinsic song
(its sound: water going down the drain
according to my friend, an Italian,

after riding in a compartment of Americans
gurgling all the way from Florence to Rome).
Why not a convoluted scheme
of intricately wrought meter and rhyme?
So what if the Hebrew has no strict patterns?
Aim for a parallel sublime;

aren't poems *for* the impossible?
Though perhaps yours wouldn't have been written
had you known how daunting their task was;
you had no Hebrew, used the Coverdale,
Wyatt, Geneva Bible, as cribs for Latin,
even *psaumes de David, mis en rime Françoise* . . .

Clearly, your secret weapon was ignorance,
also useful (look at me!) in writing a poem,
your psalms fourth- and fifth-hand half the time.
Unless (of course!) your stroke of brilliance
was to focus on the one thing you could do:
Sing and let your song be new

which they are, profoundly, even to me,
who know so many bits of the originals
of what you claim you're "translating" by heart.
Still, I'll be reading along, alternately
put-off and spellbound by your art-
ifice, when my wary eye suddenly falls

on something both completely known and new,
my own—our own—ungainly language
for a brief instant alien with grace,
a black-on-white typescript mirage
in which English letters turn into Hebrew
or at least intercept its holiness. . . .

How did you manage it, Mary?
Your contemporaries called it piety—
but I don't believe that for a second.
What motivated you was love of poetry,
or rather of your legendary
brother—lost so young—whom you would spend

your whole life working to immortalize. . . .
I'm not sure he needed you. No lighter touch
exists in English poetry than his . . .
a touch you often managed to approach
in your grief-induced lyric resolve
to force a bit of him to stay alive.

Poetry as solace, as wizardry—
and there he is, with you, all the time,
clearly palpable in all your artistry.
It was your eagerness to be with him
that kept you going back to intervene
with yet one more indomitable line,

got you through all hundred-fifty psalms.
Or maybe it was just your poet's ruse
(poetry often thrives on self-delusion)
to trick yourself to rise to his occasion . . .
Unless he just provided the excuse
to stake your own (quite vast) poetic claims.

Impossible to say from this vantage point:
to distinguish collaborator from muse,
self-doubt from false humility

but, then again, there's poetry in mystery.
Who will contradict me if I confuse
my own passions with yours—so convenient,

inevitable?—in a poem like this—
though you and I—despite the labyrinth
of misapprehension, class, religion
reinforcing our dissociation
(Jew from Christian, commoner from countess,
twenty-first century from seventeenth)

come together in passion upon passion
(forgive me Mary if dare I too far):
psalms, poetic forms, your genius brother
(I mean both the poet and the man;
no poem could manufacture that much charm).
We've even suffered from a kindred harm:

my version, albeit, fairly mild,
though I too was admonished as a child
about what a woman dared not do.
Still, I have a vast cohort, while you
were almost entirely alone.
Better yet, I had the complete Dickinson

(published just a year before I was born);
I didn't know it yet, but I had you . . .
while you had to ransack antiquity
for even fragments of poems by a woman.
But of course you weren't troubled by inequity—
it was, frankly, all you knew—

you might even have relished your position
as sole woman poet, thinker, patron—
lonely as it was—though you did encourage
your precocious niece, Mary (later Wroth).
And who can really estimate the damage
of your appalling bargain: a brother's death

required to turn you into poet?
Of course, in your time, death was everywhere;
perhaps you *were* pious—a last resort
to shore up an attenuated heart
against even further disrepair,
immersion in the psalms a sort of antidote

to life's massive overdose of pain:
from living with a sad, disfigured mother
(smallpox scars from nursing a sick queen)
mourning her husband's lost affection
to deaths of favorites—your sister, your brother,
your only daughters, Katherine, then Anne.

God made this day; he did us send it
In joy and mirth then let us spend it
excellent advice, if it would hold—
And maybe it does, when you can summon
all that air or life enfold
to distract you with a binge of exaltation . . .

or if that fails, then an assiduous
extravaganza of sublime detail
calibrated to provide the wherewithal
to face a universe we cannot alter
if not with *joy and mirth,* at least with grace:
a perfect, hand-illuminated psalter,

the loops of all its letters filled with gold—
a treasure, even, for an exacting queen—
offering a deity who'll listen
to a voice alternately humble, bold,
beseeching, thankful, ecstatic, bleak,
through which (*hallelujah,* Mary!) you still speak.

George Eliot at Cheverel Manor

Mary Anne Evans at Arbury Hall

> But I, who have seen Cheverel Manor, as he bequeathed it to his heirs,
> rather attribute that unswerving architectural purpose of his, conceived
> and carried out through long years of systematic personal exertion, to
> something of the fervour of genius, as well as inflexibility of will.
> —George Eliot, *Scenes of Clerical Life*

A homely girl in search of beauty,
she didn't have to travel far;
the (by all accounts benevolent) lady
of the estate where she was born encouraged her,

gave her free rein of the library,
whose books, no doubt, would have been enough,
but where, above her head, the extraordinary
offered its exhilarating proof

that beauty's graspable, a straightforward matter
of pairing monomania to vision.
The lucky can get by with either one
but she wasn't lucky (the too-clever daughter

of an estate agent) unless it's luck
to wander meadows at will, your daily walk
along an overgrown, wooded canal,
always within sight: a Gothic Revival

masterpiece that had been a Tudor manse,
its dark heavy panels turned to *lace-work*.
Not that she had any use for luck:
Remember? "if we had been greater, circumstance

would be been less strong against us,"
a stance at once wishful and severe,
but the very thinking that gave us *her*
whoever it is we decide she was.

Besides, what if circumstance is *for* us,
not against us? What if all
we need is one virtuoso example—
even if it's plasterwork—before our eyes,

where I, for example, always placed *her* . . .
a girl (biographers agree) like Maggie Tulliver
minus the beauty, a girl like me—
not that I wanted to drown in any river—

but she (not Maggie, but George/Mary Anne)
didn't, as a matter of fact, drown,
unless one has to drown to produce a masterwork.
Is that what she's saying? *Petrified lacework*

makes its appearance in the first,
providing not only *something of the fervour of genius*
but a pretext for self-definition—
I, she tells us, *"who have seen . . ."*

as if this George Eliot of hers
was born of knowing what can be made
of dark, ordinary Tudor manors:
Mary Anne's own *lacework petrified.*

Why *not* try what worked in Arbury Hall—
on an (Emerson's words) "serious, calm soul"
full of infinite—if inchoate—passion?
It took time, of course. First, she found religion,

renounced it, then discovered music,
then ghostwrote essays for a lover/critic
until what we might call a string of miracles
set her, at thirty-seven, writing novels

in none of which we ever find a character
in any way at all resembling her
or in all of which; George is nowhere
but Mary Anne is never very far—

there's always some version of the misfit woman
with an endless store of misdirected passion
she must work to minimize or harness;
even Alcharisi loses her voice

and gives up a preeminent career
to marry well and be a mother.
I used to think Eliot stingy, even cruel
to her heroines, not a single girl

achieves anything like her own success;
many readers think Alcharisi monstrous,
giving up—then heartless to—her firstborn son.
But perhaps that story was Eliot's own:

losing her voice her own great worry,
the price of her success far too high;
perhaps she regretted not having children.
For all we know she had an abortion

(she lived in Victorian England with a married man)
or maybe she couldn't bear to subject her characters
to the self-contortion beyond all recognition
required to effect the sort of tour de force

that became her trademark. Where was Mary Anne
beneath the exquisite plasterwork of George?
Perhaps she really did have to submerge
all traces of herself; to drown

like the character with whom she's most identified
in order to achieve what she achieved,
maybe she saw her own life as unlived
or, rather, cut off, then petrified

in masterpiece after masterpiece.
Who'd have believed her if she'd tried to write
about learning Greek and Latin, translating Strauss,
much less making the finite infinite?

No wonder she always thought she'd fail.
Hers was the sober version of the fairy tale
that Mary, in *Middlemarch, had well by heart,*
unencumbered by the far-fetched part

where the panicked mother gets to keep her child.
She paid dearly for the freak, remorseless grace
that spun a universe of straw to gold,
its dark, ungainly matter into lace.

Golden Oldie

Even now, I can't hear the organ intro
to Percy Sledge's sultry *when a man*
loves a woman without that afternoon
returning full force: it's on the radio—
you're painting? plastering? the little bedroom
and I'm giant pregnant reading *Middlemarch*
for my Ph.D exams on the glassed-in porch—
and suddenly you crank up the volume
until the entire house begins to shake.
Don't tell me there's no such thing as happiness.
You racing down the stairs, ecstatic,
shouting *listen to this! listen to this!*
your whole heart audible, mine pumping fast.
We were young, infallible. It wouldn't last.

Late December

Who knows why these few bronze hangers-on
keep clinging to this otherwise bare tree?
All the other leaves came down easily
(an early blizzard, chased by heavy rain),
weeks ago were raked, cleared away.
It's just these withered few that stay,
autumn's keepsakes on my dim walk home.
And my father, who, left to his own devices,
would put his underwear on over his trousers
if he put it on at all, what makes him—
alternately listless, angry, scared—
so willing to be wheeled off to therapy,
where, they say, he looks at them so eagerly,
greedy for instructions, tries so hard.

Eclipses of the Moon

They say there's no trusting memory,
but where else could I have acquired this red
moon-shaped blur against a deep-black sky

simultaneously vague and vivid,
this cryptic language on my father's lips?
(I'm in a blanket in his arms; snatched from bed)

lunar eclipse, he's saying, *lunar eclipse*
guiding my still-half-asleep gaze upward,
until, just beyond his pointing fingertips,

something red elaborates each word.
Lunar means *moon,* I hear him say
(or am I just infusing what I heard

with all his later lessons in vocabulary?)
eclipse, covered by the Earth's shadow
all incomprehensible to me.

What could it mean, the Earth's shadow?
and how would it reach across the sky?
There's nothing of the telltale crescendo

or decrescendo (the essential quality—
I'll learn—of an eclipse). It's instantaneous;
I'm in a blanket; my father's holding me

and pointing to the sky; I hear his voice.
It's the middle of the night and we're outside,
the sky's red blur almost extraneous—

except that only it could ever provide
the occasion for such an outsized memory.
Could there be a luckier child

than the one whose father—even when she's three—
can't bear for her to miss something wonderful?
It must have been March thirteenth, 1960.

I searched for total lunar eclipses visible
from Philadelphia (there's no red glare
if the lunar eclipse isn't total).

I was eight before the next one would occur
and by then didn't need *eclipse* defined;
there'd been a solar eclipse the year before

when I so worried about going blind
I wouldn't even approach a curtained window
until I knew danger was at an end.

But a moon's eclipse is pure bravado
on the heavens' part, at its most emphatic
an innocuous, one-night-only show,

and more of a celestial practical joke
than anything else when it's just partial;
I can remember doing a double take

at a crescent moon—*wasn't the moon just full?*—
on the last night of camp; we'd stayed awake
all night, already mourning our magical

utopian respite on the lake
from a world we loathed for its conformity.
This was precisely one year after Woodstock—

August seventeenth, 1970—
a partial eclipse visible from New England—
two days after my fourteenth birthday

and I was the sort of adolescent,
a would-be poet in the Age of Aquarius,
who cared if the moon was full or crescent,

regarding, more or less, the entire universe
as a personal communiqué to me,
ecstatic when, an hour before sunrise

the moon was full again, and dormant memory
(a blanket, my father pointing to the sky,
his voice saying *eclipse*) came surging back to me

as it did last night, though it was cloudy
and I couldn't see the promised eclipse at all:
instead, that vague red blur against the sky,

a moon from full to crescent back to full—
one atop the other, like an overlay
transparent, in a textbook—against the dull

low-hanging, heavy, winter gray,
fifty years since that full, forty since that partial—
the only eclipses of the moon that I

have managed in all these years to see
though I did point my daughters toward the sky
on numerous occasions, most recently

—it was near my birthday, so they humored me—
the most spectacular Perseids in decades.
All three drove up the canyon with me, lay

on a ratty blanket, tilted back their heads
and even joined my ecstatic oohs and aahs
without irony for once (motherhood's

for me become a matter, more or less,
of providing fodder for jokes; at least they're funny)
when one atop the other, simultaneous

twin meteors expended on the sky
their incandescent, one-time-only banners—
so fleeting and improbable that I

wouldn't have believed, without my daughters,
I'd seen what I had seen: almost a proof
that there exists a music of the spheres.

What other music could have carried off
that thrillingly unlikely pas de deux?
so indelible that if I live long enough

to outlast, as my father has, lucidity
—his answer to every question: *ask Evelyn*—
those twin shooting stars will single-handedly

intercept my mind's spreading oblivion
with their evanescent double arc.
That's what he says to me: *ask Evelyn,*

or, sometimes: *ask my wife.* It's too much work
for him to remember she's my mother;
some connective apparatus has gone dark.

But he does know that he's my father,
his face when he sees me something splendid
(his expression now an open bellwether

of what is going on inside his head);
and it's infectious, that perfect joy;
so I feel it too—however mitigated—

would almost welcome this endearing envoy
from my pre-history, this left-field chance
to know my father as a little boy,

if it weren't so absurdly out of sequence,
so heartbreakingly immutable.
Besides, he always had a kind of innocence,

marveled at a world he saw as full
of endless opportunities for wonder . . .
and though a bit afraid of the natural

(a true city kid, more at home with cinder-
blocks and cement than trees and grass)
was always after showing us the splendor

of this magical (if deadly) universe—
though he took no chances, preferred his ocean
from the undertow-free vantage point of shores,

every excursion an occasion
for still more lessons in vocabulary.
At the ocean, for example: *horizon*:

the line where the ocean meets the sky
confounded me summer after summer.
I saw no line or even opportunity

for a rendezvous of water and air
though I was enthralled by the idea.
And then, when I was what? in junior

high school, he began stuffing me
with words he'd circle in every article
of *Time* magazine: *zenith, probity,*

clandestine, assiduous, apocryphal....
Even now certain words I come across
regardless of their contexts will still

assert themselves in my father's voice:
juxtapose, harbinger, alacrity....
I've passed them on to my daughters, their ace

SAT scores my father's legacy.
Why not try his game on him?
What's largesse, Daddy? Generosity.

He barely skips a beat. *Opprobrium?*
Public disgrace. Abjure? Abstain,
each precise, well-chosen synonym

a perfect marvel of illumination
in an otherwise unbroken spell of shadow.
It's as if I've found a pristine lexicon

in the rubble of an earthquake or tornado,
every other household item lost.
Unless my father—incommunicado,

and not, manifestly, at his best—
is still himself, in there somewhere. Perhaps
his mind's just resting: a palimpsest

in the hiatus between manuscripts—
the first rubbed out, the second not yet written.
Whoever heard of an eclipse

wholly immune to orbit or rotation
moving straight from partial into full?
Meanwhile, word and definition,

twin meteors, tail on top of tail,
interrupt the darkness in unison
and I'm the witness-daughter in their thrall,

all of memory the fleeting outline
of that split-second interregnum
between the obscure and the uncertain

from my first foray into nighttime:
a blanket, my father's arms, cold air,
his finger pointing to something dim . . .

to this articulate, beseeching blur
(suspended as the meteors take aim)
reconfiguring my father's stare
as Earth's long shadow eclipses him

CPSIA information can be obtained
at www.ICGtesting.com
Printed in the USA
FFOW04n1801261214
9835FF